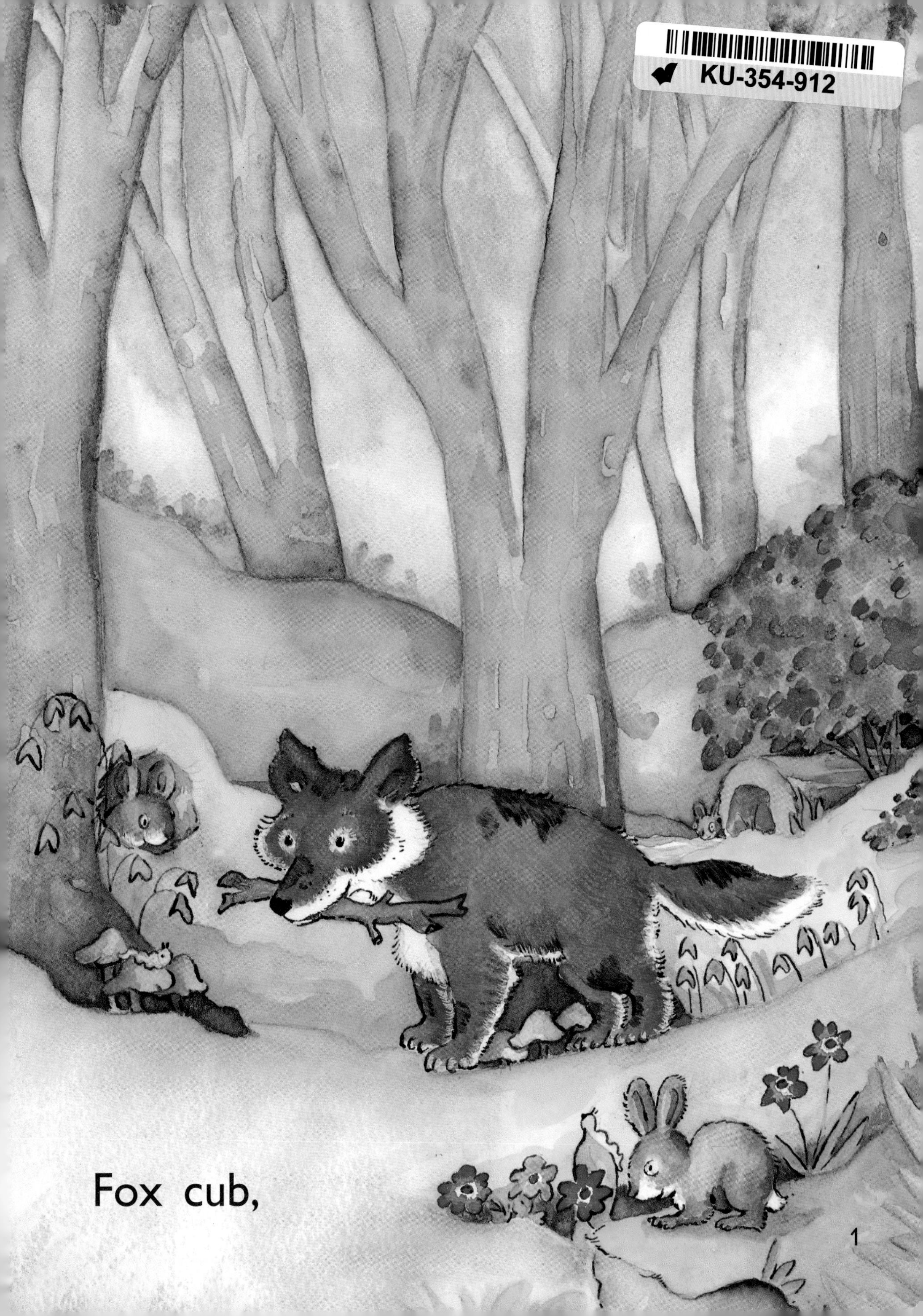

Fox cub,

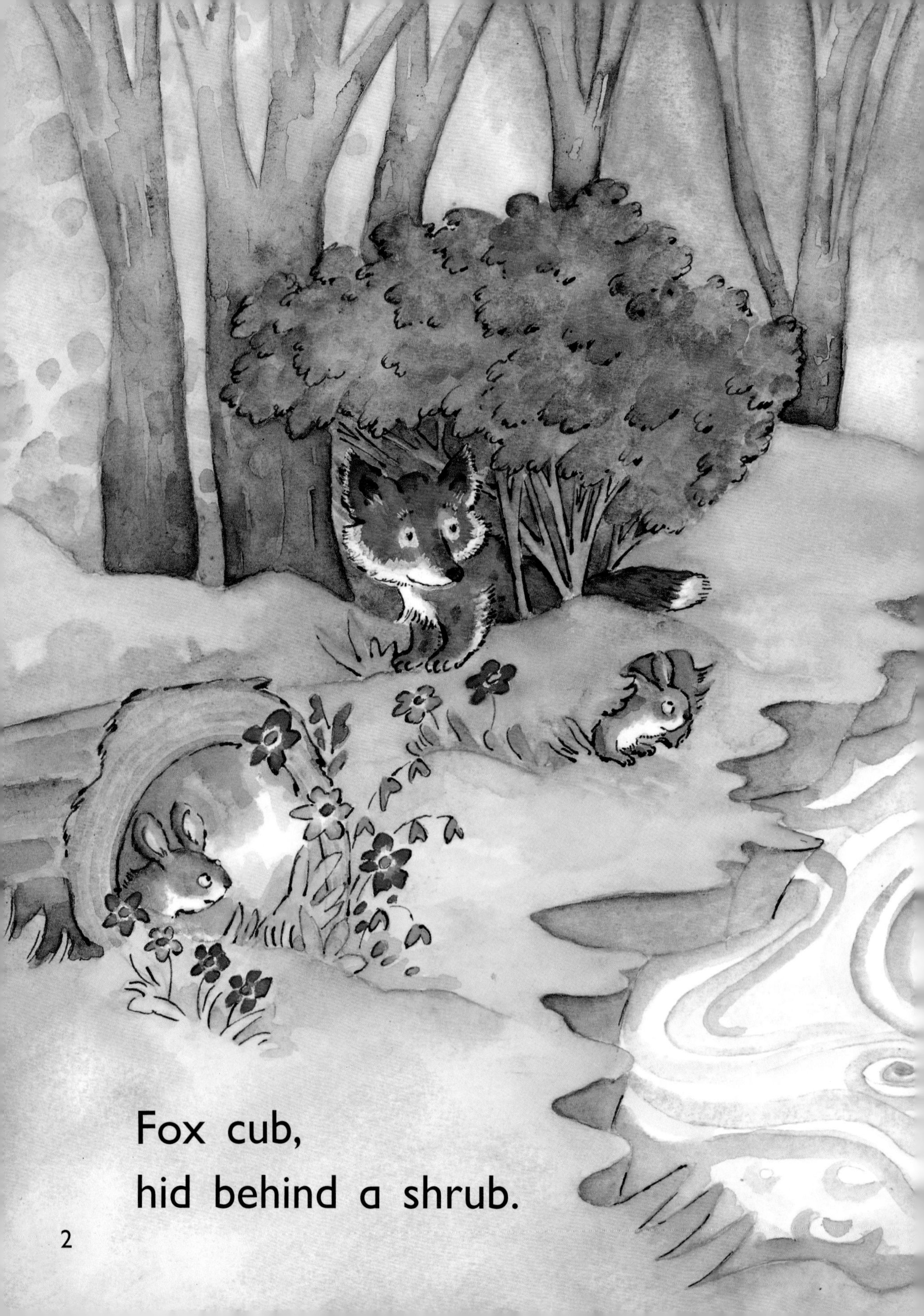

Fox cub,
hid behind a shrub.

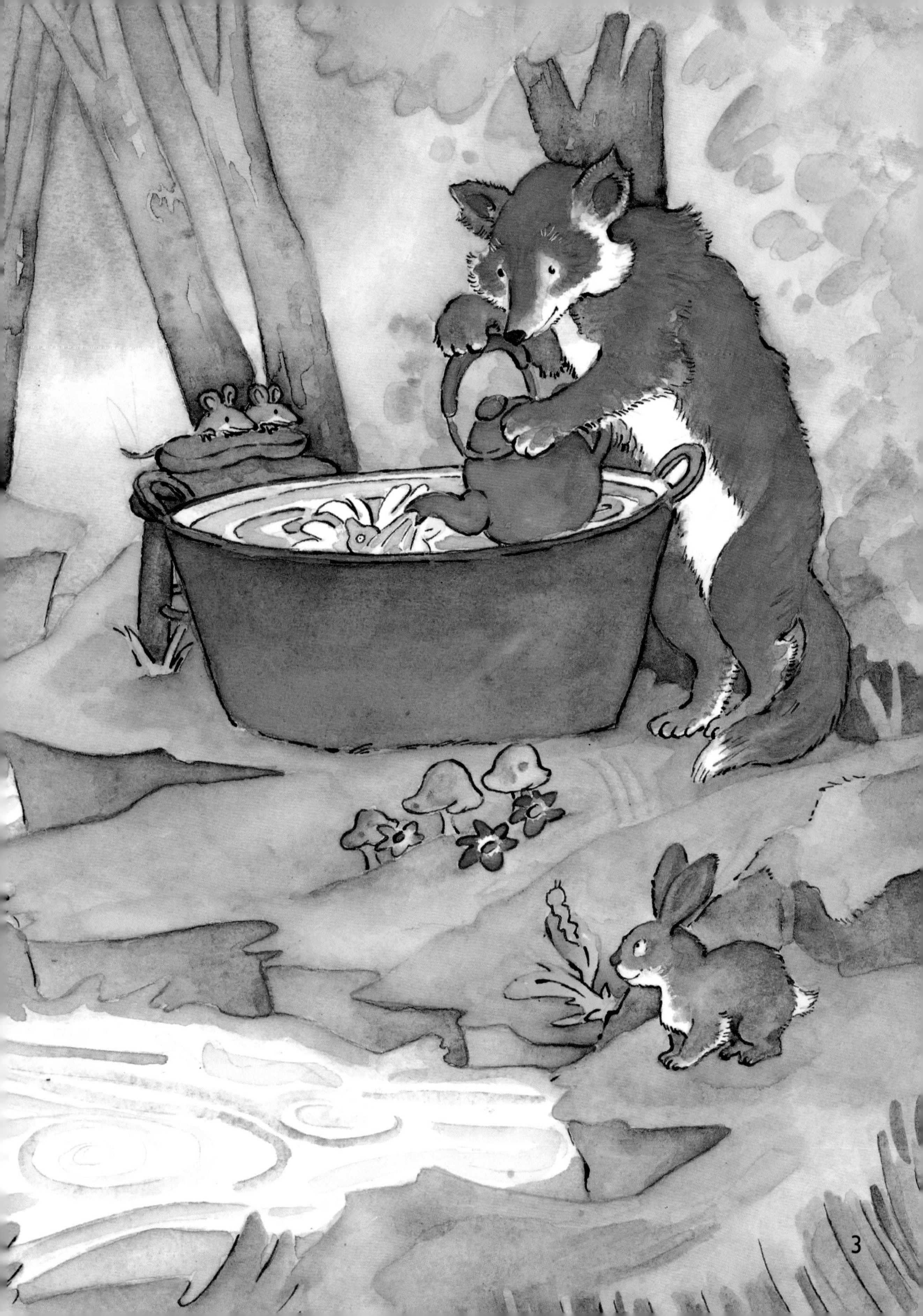

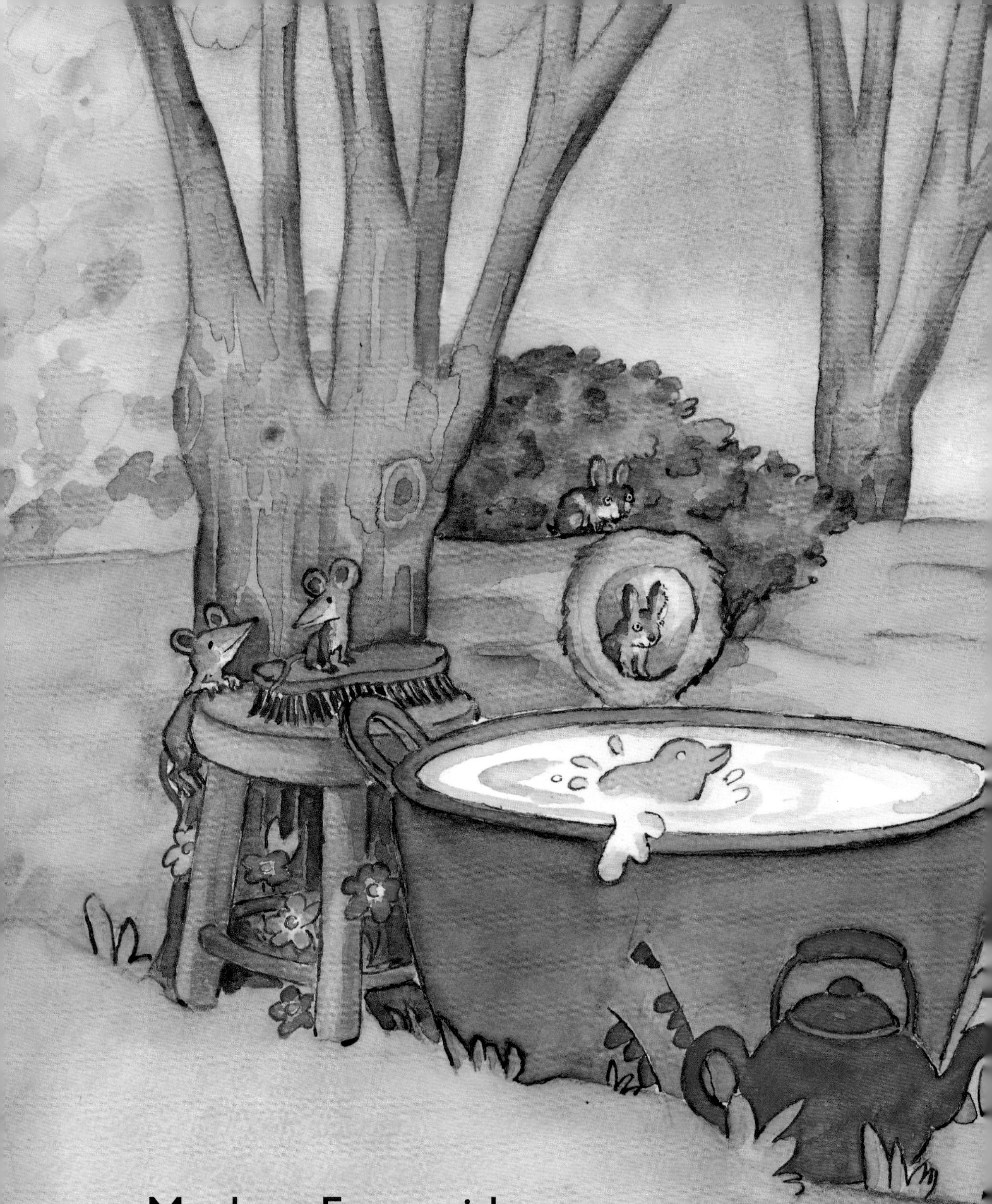

Mother Fox said,
'It's time for a scrub!'

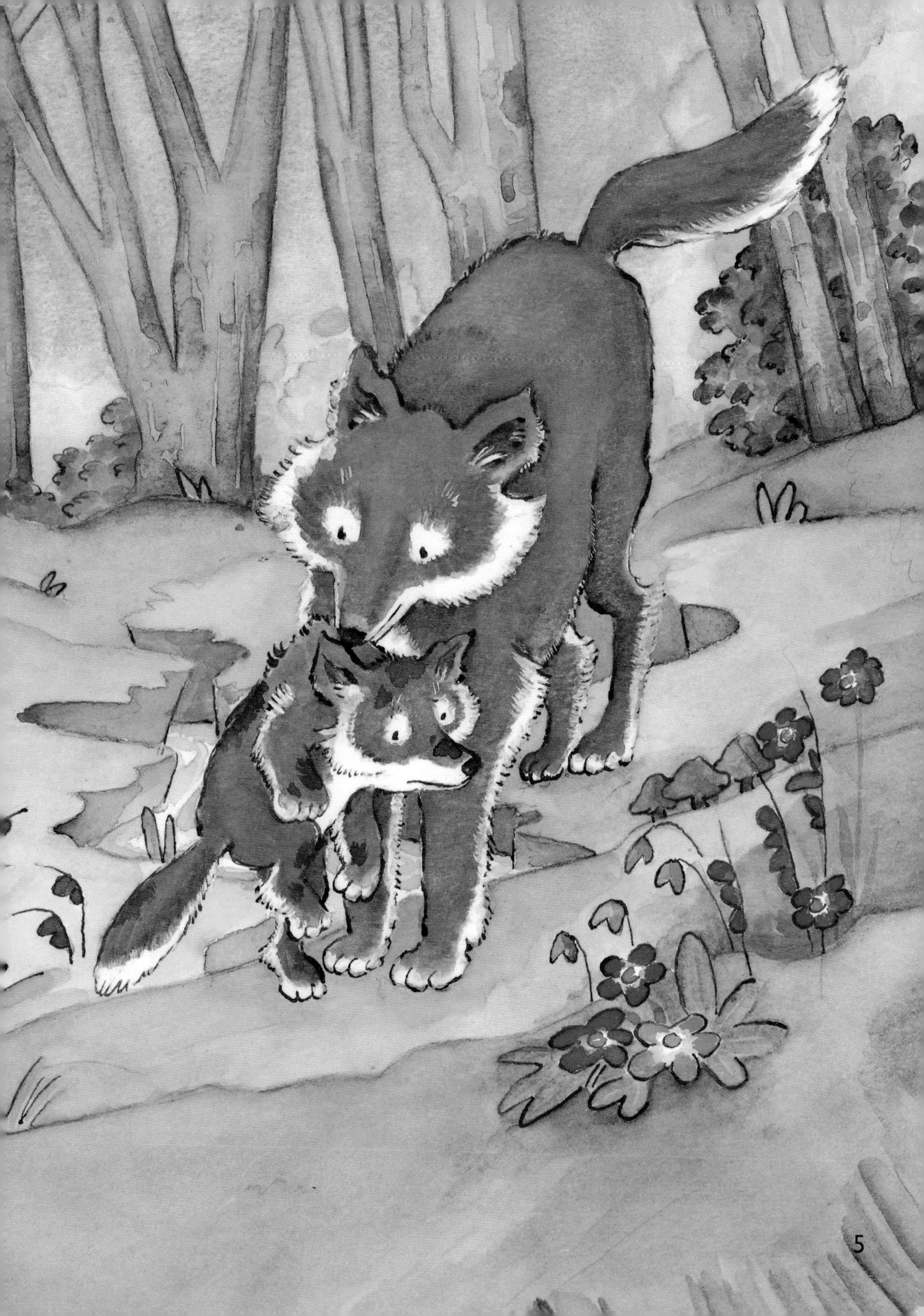

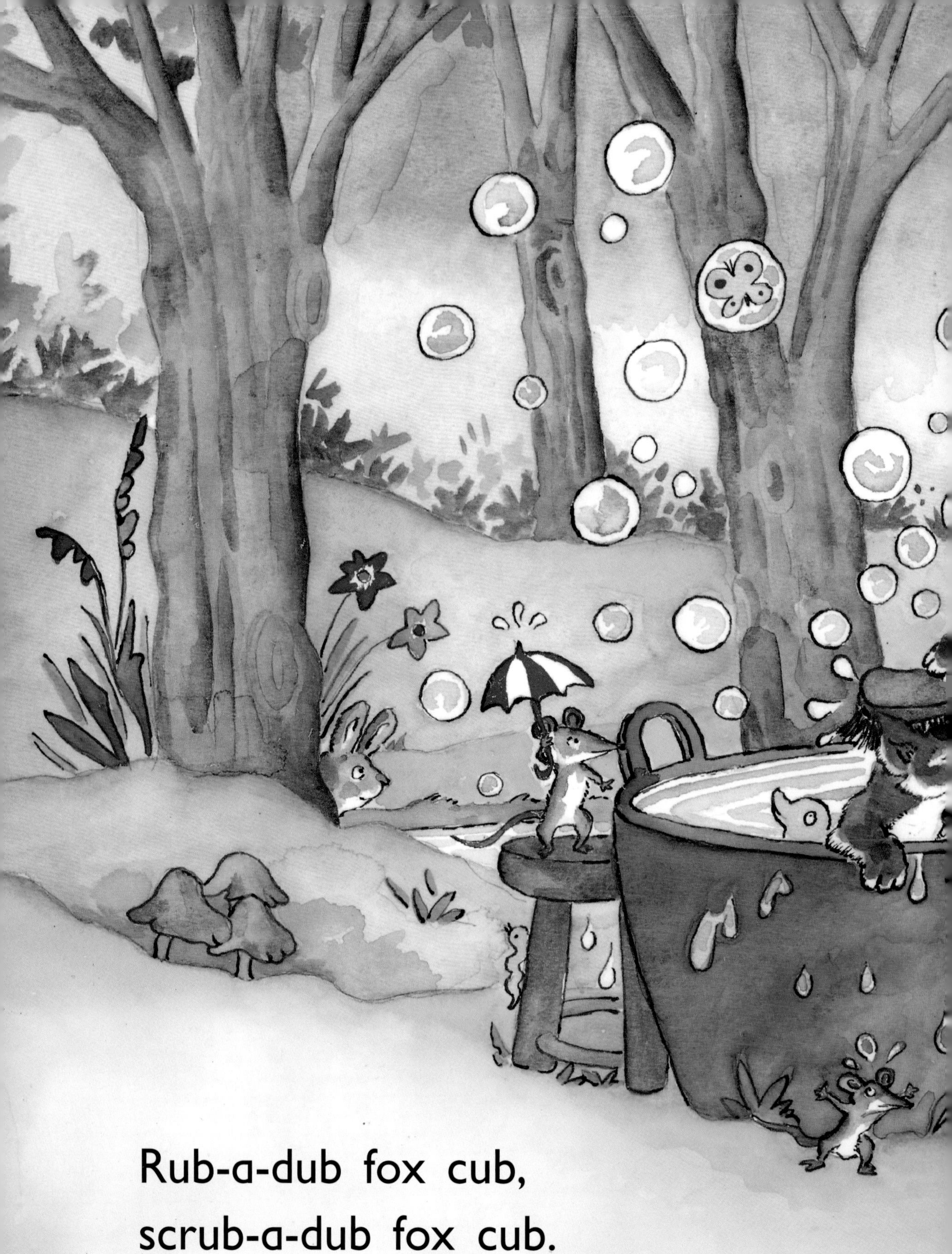

Rub-a-dub fox cub,
scrub-a-dub fox cub.

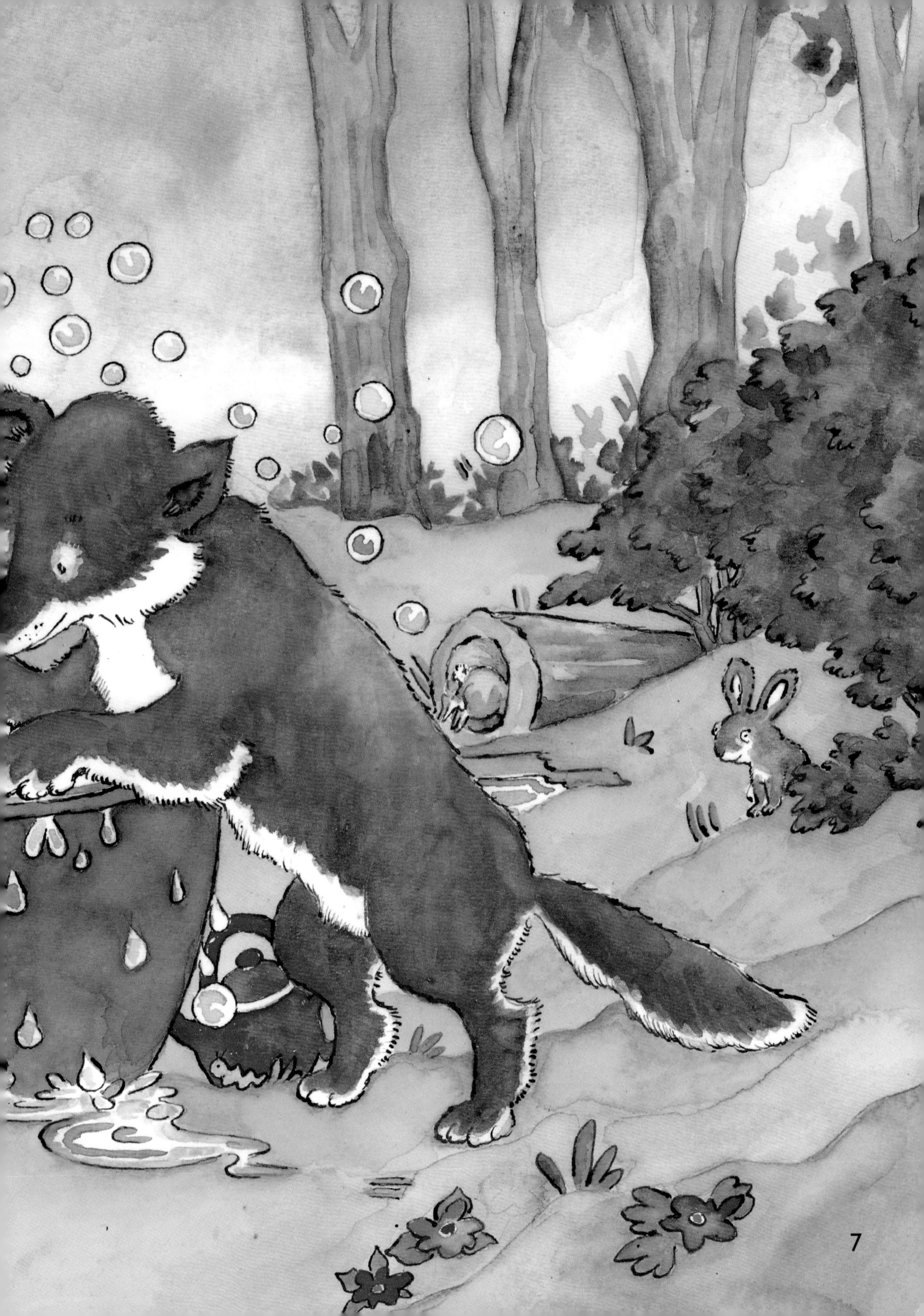

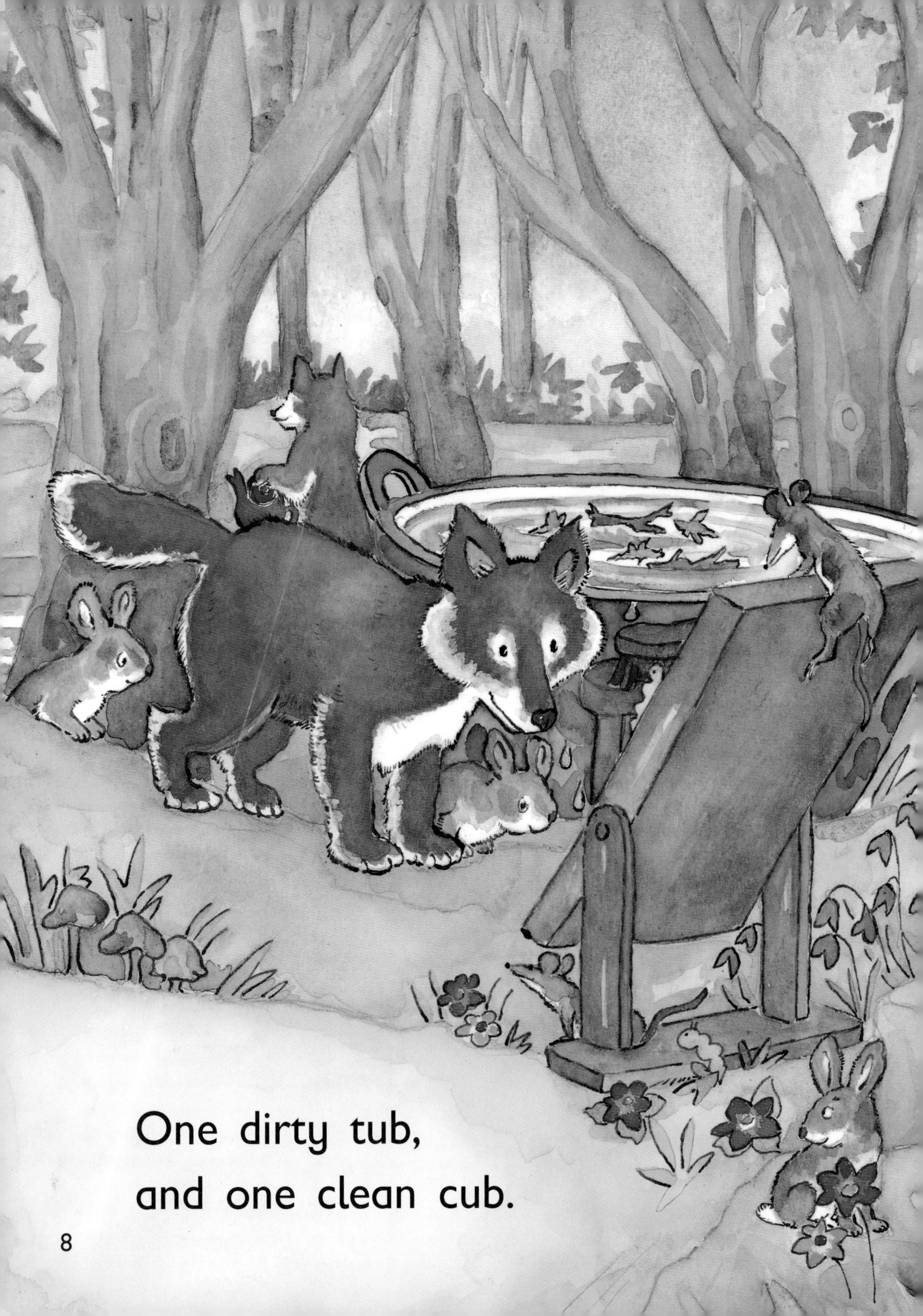

One dirty tub,
and one clean cub.